Awkward Musings

Allaysia Varnado

Awkward Musings © 2022

Allaysia Varnado

All rights reserved.

No part of this publication may be
reproduced, stored in a retrieval system, or
transmitted, in any form or by any means,
electronic, mechanical, photocopying,
recording or otherwise, without the prior
written permission of the presenters.

Allaysia Varnado asserts the moral right to
be identified as the author of this work.

Presentation by *BookLeaf Publishing*

Web: www.bookleafpub.com

E-mail: info@bookleafpub.com

ISBN: 9789357211505

First edition 2022

This book is dedicated to anyone who didn't
believe in me or my worth.

Just buy the Damn Crop Top

Just buy the damn crop top, don't try to justify it.
Ignore all the haters, the opinions and the
remarks, you are magnificent, a perfect work of
art.
Clothes are just that, clothes.
Just buy the damn crop top you know you'll look
good in, create that ensemble, like you imagined
you would.
Just buy the damn crop top, wear it with pride,
and walk down the streets with some pep in your
stride.
Just buy the damn crop top, no one will make
fun of you, and if they do, laugh because your
life has just begun.

CannaPower

Twenty minutes pass, you start to feel fuzzy,
hazzy, slightly dizzy, amazing and lovely.
The room starts to slow and your movements do
too, then you start to wonder, "Is this just you?"
You're scrolling through Tik Tok, everything
suddenly becomes funny as hell, you're laughing
hysterically, gasping for breath and sweaty as
well.
That one little gummy made you feel so nice,
you start to think of your new found sweet vice.
A few hours pass, you're brought back to the
ground, drifting off to sleep, to prepare for the
next round.

They call me...Pain

Living on edge at all times, never truly knowing
when life will be interrupted.
Living in fear of waking with that oh so familiar
pain in my head.
Sometimes it gets so bad, I wished I were...you
thought I was gonna say dead?
But in all seriousness, that throbbing, aching,
stabbing, burning feeling, sometimes it lingers
like a free loading friend.
If you're gonna stick around for days at least be
useful.
As I wait, I rock back and forth in a dark, cold
room, hoping and praying my life returns to
normal.
"Tomorrow"
If only I can hold on until tomorrow.

Depression

It's like this constant feeling of being pushed
down under a strong current.
Every time you feel it let you go, you breathe,
but you're pushed back down under.
It's like you're constantly hiding, ducking and
dodging and unknown pursuer.
You're constantly in a race against time, but you
don't know where the finish line lies.
It's like a sharp pain in your chest, throbbing and
aching, never letting up.
You feel lonely, alone even in a group of people.
"What do you have to be depressed about?" they
ask.
"Everything."

Fighting the Urge

I'm fighting the urge to cut my hair, cut away the
dead ends, the broken promises, the lost years,
the laziness, the unfulfilledness, the hurt, the
shame, the guilt.
I am fighting the urge to cut my hair, to start
fresh, anew, to be a better person, to enter 30
with a bang, finally to thrive.
I am fighting the urge to cut my hair, to let go of
things I cannot change, to let go of people who
do not deserve space in my life, to forgive those
who have done me wrong.
I am fighting the urge to cut my hair, I am losing
the battle, the start of a new beginning.

New Natural

"Don't use oil" "no rubber bands" "don't leave
styles in too long" "no chemicals"
So many rules and regulations to this whole
natural thing.
Which is right? Which advice is best?
Protective styles, braids, weaves...There are so
many ways in which we can wear our crown.
Scared to do the wrong thing and end up in
ruins, picking up the pieces of shed hair and
knots that would surely grace your bathroom
sink.
So many methods, I am confused.
Wanted is just a safe space to experiment and try
new things without being called out; what
happened to "do you"?
You "do you" and I will "do me"

That don't sit right with me

Something about this don't sit right with me, it
don't make sense
Why do we throw ourselves into a job
wholeheartedly
Why do we while our time away for pennies
only to have no recovery time.
Why do we allow ourselves to become depleted
of energy so easily
Why do we love those who don't love as fiercely
or as deeply as we love them
Something about all of that, don't sit right with
me
Why should I have to choose between groceries
or heat, gas or co pays, the dollar menu or
veggies
Does this sit right with y'all?

That key

Man, when I put that key in that door, I'm ready
to relax.
Bra on the bathroom floor, wig in the chair,
socks on the floor, face washed.
Don't call my phone after I hit that bed, it's a
sure-fire way to make me see red.
Edible popped, on my way to a far away land,
drifting away, floating on sand.
Then comes the drop, the giggles, the munchies,
then the stomachache.
Would I do it again, of course.
I don't have long to wait
A new day is here, the work day was fun, when I
put that key in the door, it's over, it's done.

Zeros

What am I doing with my life...
Working with the littles is not it
As I approach 30 I realize I hate working.
Working makes me sick
Working makes me tired
Working makes me stressed
Working brings on migraines
Why do we do it then!?
Why torture myself further, I'll quit, thats it I'll
quit.
Become a recluse, get creative, start sewing...it'll
be great, but... Bills
They never stop coming, then you're buried
under that mountain of paper with zeros. Those
zeros taunt you, they haunt you, they break you
and bend you into submission.
There's gotta be another way

My One

I never thought I would find the one whose smile would make me whole.
Whose warm embrace and playfulness would make me feel at home.
I am grateful for the one I've found and who in turn has found me, Our souls are forever tied together for all of eternity.

In Need of a Career Change

I wish I could say my current career is super
rewarding and life changing. Isn't that what
everyone wants out of a job?
But I can't, I hate it and that's ok.
I hate the way the bells ring every 40 minutes, it
urges my soul. It yanks at my nerves and it
jumbles my brain to the brink of migraines
The constant "good morning" I am forced to
utter before 8:30am is bone breaking, it is the
bane of my existence.
As I lunch in, I trade my given me for a new
one, "Ms."
The sound of crushing plastic water bottles and
the occasional loud wail brings me out of my
reverie , the only peace I have is when I am in
the clouds.
Another life beckons, it calls to me so sweetly
like a siren's song, If only I could decipher the
direction, but oh there's the bell again, duty calls.

I'm Sorry

"I'm sorry" I always seem to say that often
Why do I constantly find myself apologizing for
having a voice and opinion, for simply being
me?
Walking through life at a snail's pace, don't get
too close to anyone "I'm sorry", there it is again.
Apologizing for taking up space now, do I really
always feel like such a waste?
Trauma is hard to reverse
Growing up, the feeling of being wrong, or
afraid of being perceived the wrong way triggers
this immediate response of "I'm sorry"
The day when I can finally break free from the
"I'm sorry" will be a day to celebrate. I will take
up space, I will say what I want, I will do what I
want without fear...
Until that day comes, "I'm sorry" for not being
there yet.

Rona, go the hell away

Such a dark period in time, destruction and pain
ever present. Somber moods have been the
norm.
Sickness, death vaccines, that's all we hear about
lately
When will we be free? Is it even an option
anymore?
When will people wake and take control of this
situation, don't be too hasty, for that will draw
things out even more. Mask up, stay safe, keep
calm, but remember to live life in a new way.
Whatever was "normal", now we must adapt to a
new normal, one in which we come together,
one in which we care for one another and this
planet, one in which we can all thrive. Soon
come, soon come.

The Girl

I see a girl, shrouded in darkness, giving more of
herself than she receives.
A girl who's desperately trying to cling to life
with all she has.
A girl who gets knocked down, disappointed and
depressed...
In that same girl I see beauty, grace, a toughness
that she doesn't realize just yet
I see compassion, determination.
That girl is so many, that girl is me.
Which side will win?

Kings and Queens

The power in this world belongs to the world's
protectors, the true kings and queens.
My melanated brothers and sisters, there will
come a day when we realize who we truly are,
what we are capable of and what we really could
be.
There will come a time when we will no longer
have to choose between who gets to eat and who
doesn't.
There are seats at the table for us all.
There will come a time when we have to
demonstrate true kindness and compassion,
something that wasn't always shown to us.
Yet, like the true kings and queens of this world,
we will do it with grace, nobility and all of our
heart.
I don't know about you but I am ready for this,
it's coming, it'll be here before you know it.
Stay safe, live on, and remember to rise up when
it's time.

Absence

I wish I could love you
I wish I knew you better.
I wish I didn't have to feel a sort of sadness
when we speak.
I wish I meant it when I say I love you, but I
don't know you.
I don't feel emotionally safe, I don't feel love, I
feel tolerated.
I am not them, they are not me.
I just wish you understood how much I needed
you for stability
My story is not unique, and for that I am truly
sorry.
Your story is my story.
The pain never really goes away, you know. You
just learn to live with it and as the years go by
you learn to live without him and you'll find that
you'll thrive.

A little bit of pessimism

I should have never uttered those words "I can't
wait to grow up"
What the hell was I thinking? Life is spent like a
cycle on a washing machine, wash-rinse-repeat.
You work everyday, all week, only to make
enough to live paycheck to paycheck without
being able to save, go on vacations or enjoy the
simple pleasures of living life.
This is really not supposed to be such a sad
poem, just one to open your eyes.
Not everyone lives this way, you may say I am
complaining and that's fine, but this is how it is,
this is life for so many people.
Life is pain, but it better not be too much pain,
because who can pay a co pay in 2022, not I.
This was my little bit of pessimism for the day,
now that I've gotten it out, hopefully there will
only be optimistic thoughts from now on.

Stop giving a fuck

I'm gonna stop giving a fuck.
It seems like the appropriate thing to do
Why care about things that don't serve you?
I'm going to stop giving a fuck,
why let people make me cry, girl if you don't dry
those tears and hold that head up high.
I'm going to stop giving a fuck, they really don't
care about you, take your vacation days, travel,
fuck school.
I'm going to stop giving a fuck,
why does it seem so hard, why am I easily
affected so, easily emotionally scarred?
I am going to stop giving a fuck, I really really
want to, baby steps, one at a time, it'll come
you'll see, it's true.
I am going to stop giving a fuck, maybe not right
now, but just give me time, maybe tomorrow is
that day.

www.ingramcontent.com/pod-product-compliance
Lightning Source LLC
LaVergne TN
LVHW021346200726
843509LV00014B/2703